Travel
Smart

By Laura Buller

CELEBRATION PRESS
Pearson Learning Group

Contents

Imagine It!

Imagine that with a snap of your fingers you could zoom across the country or around the world. Where would you choose to go? What would you like to see and do? Would you stay for a day, a week, or even longer?

This book will show you how to plan for a trip. Use your imagination. Planning a trip can be almost as much fun as going on one!

Where will you choose to go on your trip?

Choose Where to Go

The first step in planning a trip is choosing a **destination**. Whether you plan to travel close to home or far away, your journey begins here. Get ready, get set, and decide where you will go!

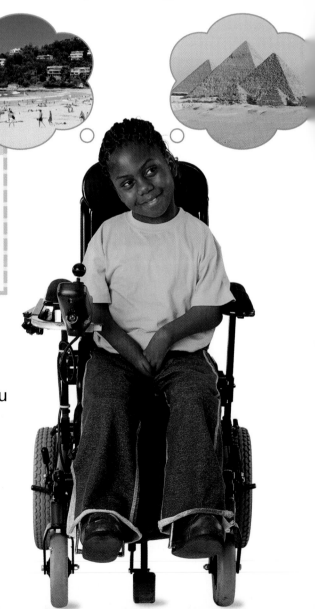

Materials

- travel or outdoor magazines
- a **globe** or an **atlas**
- a computer connected to the Internet

Steps

1 Think about what you would like to do on your trip. Do you want to ski or go to a beach? Is a trip to a big city your idea of fun? Maybe you would like to visit a famous building or other special place.

2 Look for places where you can do these things. Visit the library for ideas. Look at a globe or an atlas. Browse through travel and outdoor magazines. Ask friends and neighbors.

3 Learn more about these places. Find where they are on a **map** or in an atlas. Ask an adult to help you browse the Internet for information. Now all you have to do is choose your favorite place.

Use a Map

You can learn how to use a map well by pretending you are going on a short trip in your own town. You could plan a trip to a park, museum, or to the library. You'll begin by finding your own street on the map.

Materials

- a road map of your town
- two rulers
- paper and a pencil

Steps

1 Spread out the map on a table or on the floor. Look for the list of street names on the map. This list may be on the other side.

2 Find the name of your street on the list. Beside it will be a letter and a number. Write them on a sheet of paper.

Mast Road	B5
Mill Street	E5
Ocean Way	A3
Park Avenue	B5
Pleasant Street	D1
Tree Road	E3
Vine Gardens	A2

3 Now look along the edges of the map. You will see letters on one edge and numbers on another edge. They form a grid. Find the letter and the number of your street.

4 Find where the lines come together. Use the rulers to help you. Hold the rulers along the lines. Your street is inside the square where the two lines meet.

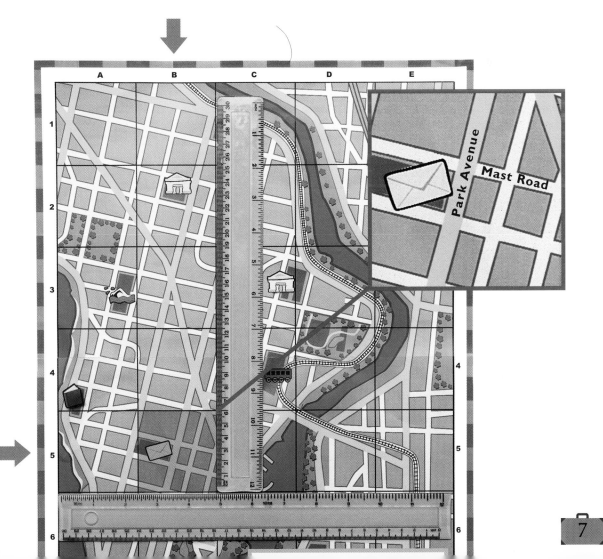

Plan a Route

Now that you've found your own street on the map, you can choose where you'd like to go. A map will help you plan a **route**, or way, to your destination. This activity will show you how to plan your route.

Materials

- a road map of your town
- a ruler
- a pencil
- a long piece of string

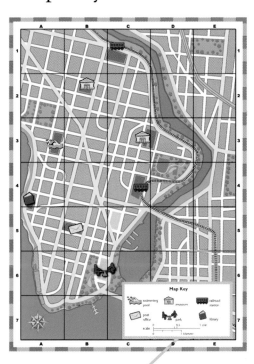

Steps

1 Choose a place to visit. Look at the **symbols** in the **map key** on your map. These symbols may help you find a place to visit, such as a park or a museum.

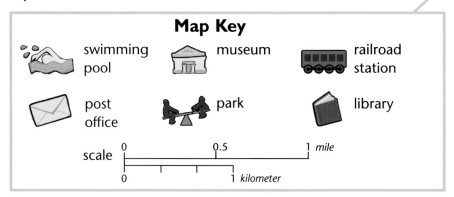

Map Key

swimming pool

museum

railroad station

post office

park

library

scale

0   0.5   1 *mile*

0   1 *kilometer*

2 Use the grid lines on the map to find that place. You'll find it the same way you found your street. Draw a circle around it.

3 Choose roads that connect your street to the destination. There are usually several different roads you can choose. Then draw a line along the roads between the two **locations**, or places. This will be your route.

4 Now you will find the length of your route. Place a piece of string along the route. Mark the string at both ends.

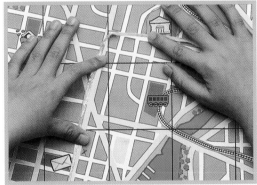

5 Find the map **scale**. The scale helps you figure out the distance between two places. Inches or centimeters are often used to represent miles or kilometers.

| 0 | 0.5 | 1 *mile* |

| 0 | 1 *kilometer* |

2 inch = 1 mile, 3 centimeters = 1 kilometer

6 Place the string on a ruler. How many inches or centimeters is your route? Use the map scale to find out how many miles or kilometers that equals.

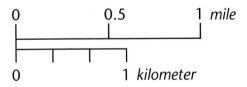

Find the Right Transportation

When traveling close to home, you might walk, ride your bike, or ride in a bus or car. However, you might take a trip with family or friends that is farther away. You can help find the right transportation.

Materials

- a computer connected to the Internet
OR
- transportation prices and **schedules**

Steps

1 Choose two ways you could get to your destination. You could take a bus, boat, train, or airplane.

train and bus schedules

2 Ask an adult to help you find transportation prices and schedules. A schedule will tell you how long the trip will take. An adult can help you find information on the Internet or at a station or airline.

3 Look at the prices for the different types of transportation and compare them. Which form of transportation is more expensive? Which is cheapest?

4 Now look at the schedules. Find the departure times. These times tell you when an airplane, train, bus, boat, or subway leaves. Then find the arrival times. These times tell you when it arrives at the destination. What times will work best for you and your family?

You can purchase your tickets from vending machines at many stations.

5 Choose the transportation that will work best for you.

Trains can take you on short trips between cities or long trips across the country.

Ready, Set, Pack!

By now, you know where you are going and how you will get there. What should you take with you? It all depends on your destination and how long your trip will be!

Materials

- a suitcase or a backpack
- paper and a pencil
- a newspaper
  OR
- a computer connected to the Internet

Steps

1 Find out what the weather will be like. You can look up the weather in the newspaper. Ask an adult to help you use the Internet if the place is not listed in your newspaper. Remember, you may need certain clothes for hot or cold weather.

2 Make a list of things you'll need on your trip. Start with the basics.

Packing Checklist

toothbrush and toothpaste

comb ✓

clean clothes

soap and shampoo ✓

shoes and socks

camera and film

money and tickets ✓

photo ID

address book ✓

jacket

pen

journal ✓

umbrella

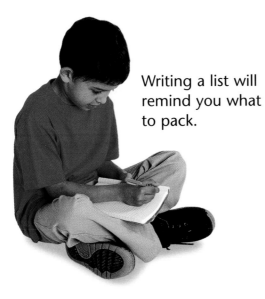

Writing a list will remind you what to pack.

3 Think about what you'll be doing on your trip. Will you need hiking shoes or a swimsuit? Add those items to your list.

4 Now start packing! Check things off as you put them in the suitcase or backpack. Put anything that might spill into plastic bags.

You will need to pack a suitcase for a trip that will be longer than a day.

Remember Your Trip

Now you know how to be a smart traveler. Before you leave, be sure to let someone know where you are going and how long you will be traveling. Now you're ready to go and have fun. Don't forget to collect some **souvenirs**. Here is how you can display your souvenirs to help you remember your trip and share it with others.

Materials

- a large sheet of posterboard
- glue or tape
- markers, paints, or crayons
- things you've collected from your trip

Steps

1 Gather the souvenirs you collected on your trip. Use things that aren't heavy such as photographs, postcards, tickets, or brochures. Spread them out on a table.

2 Arrange some of these things on the posterboard. Glue or tape them to the poster.

3 Draw or write about your favorite experiences on the poster. You could draw your favorite food and a special activity that you did. Then give your poster a title such as "My Trip to (the place you visited)."

4 Ask an adult to help you hang up your poster.

My Trip to London

Glossary

atlas   a collection of maps, usually in the form of a book

destination   the place where someone is going

globe   a round ball with a map of Earth printed on it

locations   the places where things are

map   a flat drawing that shows where things are

map key   a list on a map of all the symbols used and what they stand for

passport   an official booklet issued by the government that identifies a person

route   the path taken to get to a place

scale   the way distances are measured on a map

schedules   lists of times when trains, buses, boats, and planes arrive and depart

souvenirs   things people keep to remind them of a place they've visited

symbols   something that stands for something else